Tarantulas

by Emily McAuliffe

Content Consultant:
Dr. Robert Breene
American Tarantula Society

RiverFront Books

An Imprint of Franklin Watts
A Division of Grolier Publishing
New York   London   Hong Kong   Sydney
Danbury, Connecticut

RiverFront Books
http://publishing.grolier.com

Printed in the United States of America.

Library of Congress Cataloging-in-Publication Data
McAuliffe, Emily.
    Tarantulas /by Emily McAuliffe.
    p. cm.--(Dangerous animals)
    Includes bibliographical references and index.
    Summary: Discusses the physical characteristics, habitat, and behavior of
the poisonous tarantula.
    ISBN 1-56065-621-2
    1. Tarantulas--Juvenile literature. [1. Tarantulas. 2. Spiders.]
I. Title. II. Series.
QL458.42.T5M39   1998
595.4'4--dc21

                                        97-8342
                                          CIP
                                           AC

Photo credits
Heather Angel, 24
James C. Cokendolpher, 9, 18, 30, 34, 38, 41, 42-43
Dwight Kuhn, 6, 14, 21, 36
James P. Rowan, 8, 10, 23
Unicorn Stock, cover
Rick C.West, 26, 28, 32

Table of Contents

Fast Facts about Tarantulas

Size: Tarantulas are known for being large, heavy spiders. But the size of a tarantula depends on what kind it is. Their legspan ranges from one to 13 inches (30 to 390 centimeters).

Coloring: Tarantula species have many different colorings. They can be brown, black, red, or blue. Sometimes tarantulas have colored stripes.

Habitat: Tarantulas live in many different areas. They can live in very dry, warm, tropical, or sub-tropical climates. Tropical means hot and rainy.

Range: Tarantulas live on all continents except Antarctica. About 25 to 50 species of tarantula live in the United States. Most live in Oklahoma, Texas, Arizona, New Mexico, California, Nevada, Utah, Missouri, Kansas, Arkansas, Louisiana, and Colorado.

Food: Most tarantulas eat insects. They eat crickets, grasshoppers, and beetles. Larger tarantulas eat mice, lizards, and frogs.

Behavior: Most tarantulas are nocturnal. This means they are most active at night.

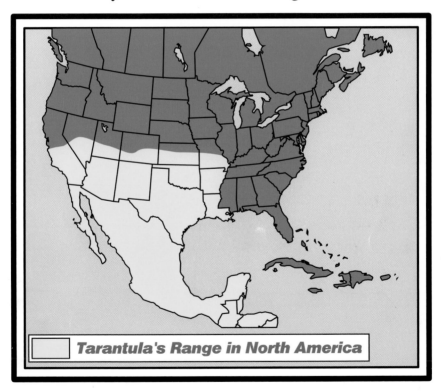

Tarantula's Range in North America

Chapter One

The Tarantula

Some tarantula species are among the largest spiders in the world. A species is a group of similar animals that can mate with each other. Tarantulas are predators. A predator is an animal that hunts another animal for food. Tarantulas kill their victims by striking from above. They hold down their victims and bite them with their fangs. A fang is a long, pointed tooth with a small hole in its end.

But it is not just fangs that kill victims. Tarantulas produce a poison called venom. When tarantulas bite, they release venom into their victims' bodies. The venom kills the victims.

Tarantulas use venom to kill their victims.

A tarantula's appearance makes some people afraid of it.

Sometimes tarantulas bite people. Usually tarantula bites are not very dangerous to people. Some tarantula species have venom powerful enough to kill people. But so far there have been no recorded human deaths caused by tarantula bites. Many people compare tarantula bites to wasp or bee stings. Most tarantula bites do not hurt for more than a few days.

Even so, it is not just tarantula venom that scares people. Many tarantulas are large and hairy. Their appearance makes some people afraid of them. Many movies show giant, hairy spiders like tarantulas attacking and killing people. But the movies are mistaken. Tarantulas are dangerous to small animals. But they do not hunt and kill people.

Tarantulas are part of the scientific class Arachnida. The Arachnida class includes all other spiders, as well as scorpions, mites, and ticks. There are about 800 tarantula species.

Tarantulas have fangs that can produce painful bites. In the 1800s, some people thought the best way to treat a tarantula bite was to rub it with hot pig fat. Today, people know this is not the best treatment. A person suffering from a tarantula bite should do several things:
1) Wash the bite with soap and water.
2) Put medicine on the bite to help protect the wound from germs.
3) Keep the bite clean so it will heal quickly.
4) Place a cool cloth over the bite to lessen its pain.
5) If the bite does not heal, visit the doctor.

Most parts of a tarantula's body are covered with hair.

Range

Tarantulas live on all continents except
Antarctica. Tarantulas can adapt to many
different climates. Many live in dry, warm, sub-

tropical, and tropical areas. Tropical means hot and rainy.

About 25 to 50 species of tarantula live in the United States. Most live in Oklahoma, Texas, Arizona, New Mexico, California, Nevada, Utah, Missouri, Kansas, Arkansas, Louisiana, and Colorado.

Appearance

Tarantula species are many different sizes. Their legspans range from one to 13 inches (30 to 390 centimeters). They have fangs that fold under their bodies.

Different species of tarantulas have different colorings. They can be purple, brown, red, black, or blue. Some species have bands of bright color on their legs.

Most parts of a tarantula's body are covered with hair. In fact, Latin Americans call tarantulas arañas peludas. Arañas peludas means hairy spiders.

An exoskeleton covers spiders. An exoskeleton is a structure on the outside of an animal. Some parts of the exoskeleton are hard

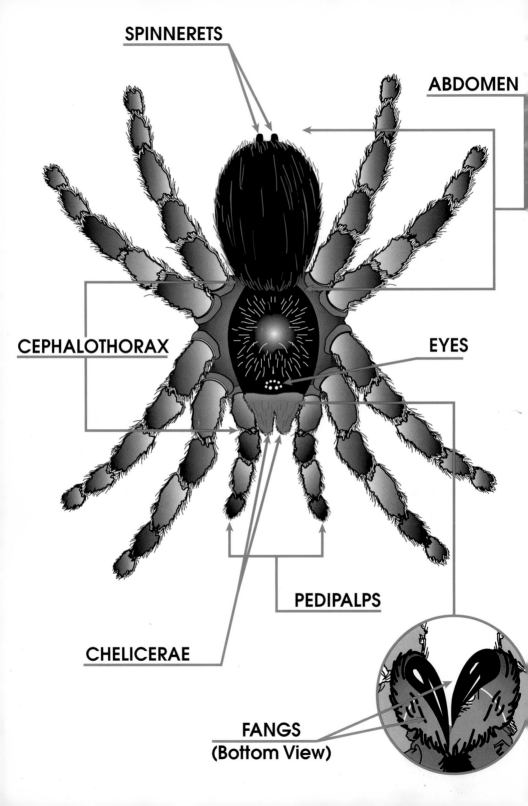

SPINNERETS

ABDOMEN

CEPHALOTHORAX

EYES

PEDIPALPS

CHELICERAE

FANGS
(Bottom View)

and some parts are soft. It helps a spider keep water in its body. An exoskeleton also helps protect a tarantula from its enemies.

The Cephalothorax

A tarantula's body has two main parts. The first part is the cephalothorax. The cephalothorax contains many organs including a tarantula's brain, eyes, head, mouth, and fangs.

There is one chelicera on each side of a tarantula's mouth. The chelicerae act like a pair of jaws. A tarantula uses its chelicerae to tear its food apart. Some tarantula species also dig with their chelicerae. A fang is part of each chelicera. A tarantula's fangs can be as long as one-half inch (about one centimeter).

One pedipalp is next to each chelicera. The pedipalps work like arms. They are about half as long as a tarantula's legs. Special hairs that help a tarantula smell and taste are on the end of each pedipalp. A tarantula uses pedipalps to find and hold food. Pedipalps also bring food to a tarantula's mouth.

All spiders have eight legs that attach to the cephalothorax. People have joints at the hip,

13

Spinnerets spin liquid silk into threads.

knee, and ankle. A tarantula's leg has seven
joints. It can bend its legs at each of the joints.

The end of a tarantula's leg has two claws
and sticky hairs. Both of these features help a
tarantula climb. Some South American, Central
American, and Asian tarantulas live in trees.

The Abdomen
The second main part of a tarantula's body is the
abdomen. It contains many organs, including a
tarantula's heart, lungs, and spinnerets.

A tarantula has spinnerets at the end of its abdomen. A spinneret is a body part that spins liquid silk into threads. Spinnerets look like tails. Organs inside a tarantula's body produce the liquid silk. Then tarantulas use their spinnerets to spin silk threads.

Senses

A tarantula has eight eyes that are located just above its mouth. Many scientists now believe a tarantula can see better than people once thought. Still, it does not have very good eyesight. During the day, a tarantula can only see things that are about three feet (90 centimeters) away. So a tarantula must also rely on its hair to help it locate moving objects. The hairs send a message to a tarantula's brain when something moves near it. Some hairs can even sense sound waves.

Scientists are not sure how well a tarantula can see during the night. They are trying to learn more about the tarantula's eyesight.

Chapter Two

Survival

A tarantula is cold-blooded. This means tarantulas receive body heat from their surroundings. In cold weather, its body cools down. In warm weather, its body heats up. A tarantula will die in areas that are too cold or too hot. Temperatures between 75 and 85 degrees Fahrenheit (23 to 29 degrees Celsius) are good for tarantulas.

Tarantulas move into the sun if they become too cold. The sun warms their bodies. They move out of the sun into cooler areas to help reduce their body temperature.

Tarantulas receive body heat from their surroundings.

Some tarantulas line their burrows with silk.

Burrows

Many spiders live in webs made of silk.
Tarantulas do not. Some tarantula species live in
trees. But many tarantulas live in underground
burrows. A burrow is a hole made by an animal
as a home. Tarantulas use their chelicerae to dig

burrows. Some burrowing tarantulas dig a straight tunnel 10 inches (25 centimeters) long. Then they curve the tunnel to the left or right. This makes an L shape. At the end of the tunnel, they dig a wider area called a den.

Sometimes tarantulas move into burrows that other animals have left. Tarantulas are not known to share their burrows with each other.

Some tarantulas use their spinnerets to line their burrows with silk. Certain species also make silk covers for their burrow entrances. Other species put piles of dirt in front of their burrows.

Tarantulas that live in warm areas stay active all year long. Tarantulas that live in colder areas cover the entrance to their burrows during cold weather. They rest inside their burrows until the weather becomes warmer.

Burrows are often moist and cool. Tarantulas spend all day in their burrows. Some spend the day peeking from their burrow entrances. If they see people, they retreat into their burrows and hide.

Many tarantulas are nocturnal. Nocturnal means active at night. They leave their burrows only at night to hunt for food. Tarantulas that live in trees most likely hunt during the day.

Food
Tarantulas are predators and scavengers. A scavenger is an animal that searches and eats another animal's left-over food.

Most of the time, tarantulas catch their own food. Tarantulas usually eat insects. They eat crickets, grasshoppers, and beetles. Larger tarantulas eat mice, lizards, and frogs. Sometimes tarantulas eat other tarantulas.

Some tarantulas do not need much food to live. If they have to, tarantulas can go without food for several months.

Hunting
Tarantulas use their body hairs to help them hunt. These hairs sense movement. Tarantulas are also sensitive to smells. They have special hairs on their legs and pedipalps that help them locate prey. Prey is an animal hunted and eaten as food.

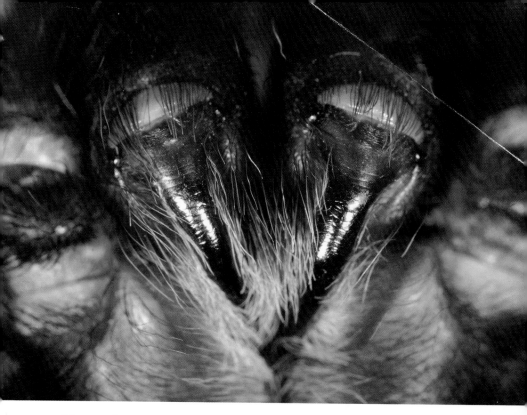

Tarantulas use their fangs to bite their victims.

Tarantulas use their eyes to help them see prey. If prey is too far away, tarantulas cannot see the animals clearly. Then they are unable to tell one animal from another.

Tarantulas grab their prey with their front legs. Then they pull prey into their chelicerae. They use their fangs to bite their victims and inject venom. Then tarantulas use their pedipalps to position their prey for eating.

Tarantulas digest food outside of their bodies. Tarantulas pour digestive juices onto their prey from special organs in their mouths. The digestive juices begin to soften the prey. Tarantulas also use their chelicerae to mash up the prey while the juices makes it soft. Then tarantulas eat the digested food from their prey's bodies.

This process can take a long time. It may take tarantulas a whole day to soften and eat small animals.

Warnings

Many animals eat tarantulas for food. Some ants may eat young spiders and spider eggs. Tarantulas have ways to protect themselves from enemies. Tarantulas in Africa and Asia are fierce. They bite when they sense danger.

Many tarantulas give warnings when they feel scared or threatened. These warnings are meant to scare away tarantulas' enemies. Tarantulas stand up on their back legs. They

Tarantulas hold their front legs in the air as a warning.

hold their two front legs up in the air and may even tap their enemies.

Another warning some tarantulas make is a hissing noise called stridulation. Tarantula

Tarantulas rub hairs together to scare their enemies.

species make this noise in different ways. Some tarantulas rub the hairs on their chelicerae and pedipalps together to make this noise. This noise may or may not scare away enemies.

Tarantulas in North America, Central America, and South America have another warning. They try to scare other animals by scraping special hairs off of their undersides. Wind blows these hairs toward tarantulas' enemies. These hairs bother the enemies' skin and eyes. Each hair has many tiny hooks and barbs that dig into soft skin.

Some scientists believe that tarantulas use these hairs in other ways, too. They think tarantulas may use the hairs to keep insects away from themselves and their eggs.

Spider Wasps

A spider wasp is a giant wasp that can grow to almost three inches (seven centimeters) long. A spider wasp is not scared by a tarantula's warnings. These two enemies will battle to the death. A tarantula will eat the wasp if the spider wasp loses the fight.

Spider wasp species use different methods to fight tarantulas. Some spider wasps just sting tarantulas wherever they can. Other spider wasps try to push tarantulas over and

sting them. The wasps may also sting tarantulas when the tarantulas' front legs are raised to fight. The wasps' stingers inject venom into the tarantulas. This venom paralyzes the tarantulas. Paralyzed means unable to move.

Some species of spider wasp will dig a nest where the tarantula was defeated. Other kinds of spider wasp will drag the paralyzed tarantula to an existing nest. Some species of spider wasp enter a tarantula's burrow and sting the tarantula. The tarantula remains paralyzed in its burrow.

Next, a wasp lays one egg on the tarantula. When the egg hatches, the wasp larva eats the tarantula alive. A larva is a young insect during its worm-like growth stage. The tarantula will die when the larva eats an important organ. Meanwhile, the tarantula remains unable to move or defend itself while the larva eats it. The tarantula might stay alive for weeks or months while it is being eaten.

Spider wasps sting tarantulas.

Chapter Three

A Tarantula's Life

Tarantulas do not mate until they are fully grown. The amount of time it takes for them to become an adult depends on their species. Some species are adult after 10 years. Others take 18 months to four years to become adults.

Some tarantulas mate between August and November. Others mate in the spring. Tarantulas that live in desert areas mate during the right weather conditions.

Male tarantulas must be careful when they approach females. Otherwise, the females may think the males are meals rather than mates. The males tap the females' legs. This calms the females. The males have special body parts that act like hooks to hold the females' fangs. That

A male will tap a female's legs before mating.

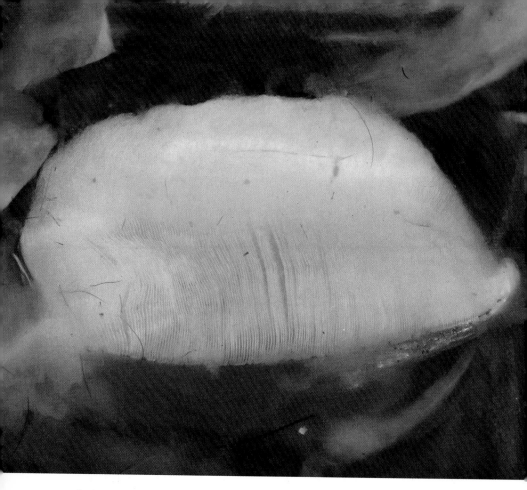

An eggsac can contain hundreds of eggs.

way, the females cannot bite the males. After mating, males must leave quickly. Otherwise, females may eat the males.

Sometimes females do not mate. If they do not mate, the eggs may dissolve in their bodies. Other times, females lay the eggs and eat them.

Eggsacs

A female that is ready to lay eggs first spins a silk pad. This pad holds hundreds of eggs. The female lays her eggs on the silk pad. A female lays about 60 to 1,400 yellowish eggs. The number of eggs depends on which tarantula species she belongs to. Each egg can produce one spiderling. A spiderling is a newborn spider.

After all the eggs are laid, the female spins another silk pad. She covers the eggs with the second pad. Then she uses more silk to seal the two pads together. This forms an eggsac. A female guards her eggsac for six weeks.

Spiderlings

Spiderlings hatch in about six weeks. The time it takes for them to hatch often depends on the weather.

Newly hatched spiderlings are white. They turn brown after a few days. Most spiderlings leave the mother within several weeks. The spiderlings must find or dig their own burrows. Species that live in trees must find their own areas of trees.

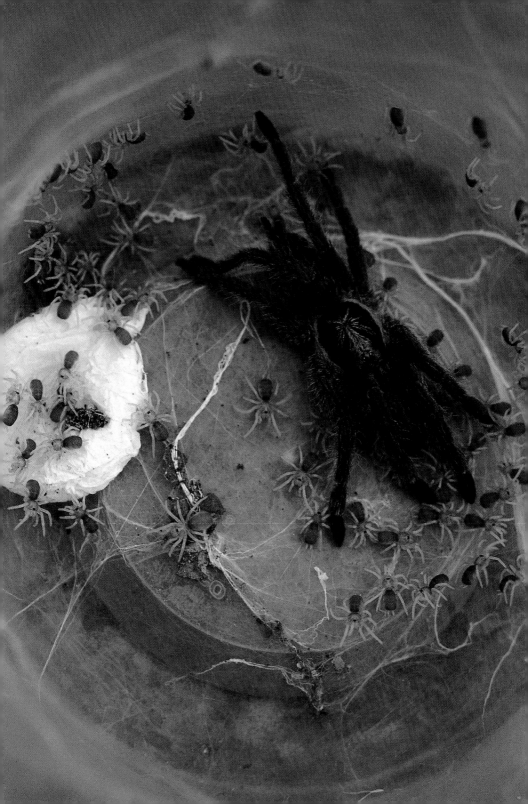

Spiderlings are small and weak. They are easy prey for enemies like scorpions and other spiders. Scientists are not sure what percentage of spiderlings live to adulthood in the wild.

Molting

Humans have a skeleton inside their bodies that is covered with soft skin. The skin stretches and allows the skeleton to grow.

Tarantulas' hard exoskeletons do not stretch and grow. Tarantulas must shed their exoskeletons as they grow. The new exoskeleton is larger than the old one. This lets tarantulas grow. This process is called molting.

Tarantulas grow new exoskeletons under their old ones. Their old exoskeletons separate from their new ones during the molt. This can take several hours. Then tarantulas roll on their backs or sides and stick their legs in the air. They squirm out of the old exoskeleton.

It takes a while for the new exoskeleton to harden. Tarantulas are very weak during this

Spiderlings are small and weak.

time. They do not have their hard covering to protect them. This makes it easy for enemies to attack.

During a molt, tarantulas can do some amazing things. Tarantulas can grow new legs if their old ones are lost or seriously damaged.

Growing spiderlings molt six to eight times each year. They molt less often as they grow older. Adult tarantulas molt only once every year. Sometimes they might even skip a year.

Males do not live long after they mate for the first time. The amount of time they live depends on the tarantula species. The time ranges from two weeks to two years after their first mating season. Adult female tarantulas live longer than males. Some female tarantulas have lived up to 20 years.

Tarantulas shed their old exoskeletons during a molt.

Chapter Four

Tarantulas and People

Some people like tarantulas so much that they keep them as pets. Popular species kept as pets include the Chilean rose and the Mexican redknee tarantulas. Most members of these tarantula species are calm and can make good pets.

Some people are worried that certain tarantula species may be in danger of becoming extinct. Extinct means an animal species has died out and no longer exists. The Mexican redknee is one of the species that has an uncertain future.

The Mexican redknee is a popular pet tarantula.

Some people are concerned because tarantulas are taken out of their homes in the wild. Tarantulas are also losing areas to live. People are building homes where tarantulas once lived. Farmers are planting crops in places that would be good for tarantula homes.

Even though wild tarantulas face problems, many scientists do not feel tarantulas are in danger. Many scientists and pet store owners breed tarantulas. There are many tarantulas born this way every year.

Pet Tarantulas

Some tarantulas can be easily hurt. This is because their abdomen is weak. Tarantulas could die if they fall or are dropped. Their abdomen might split open when they hit the ground. Tarantula species that live in trees are a little stronger. They do not get hurt as easily.

Some people think it is best not to hold a tarantula at all. This protects both the spider and the owner from harm. People who do

People who handle tarantulas should be careful.

handle tarantulas should be gentle and careful with the spiders.

Future

People need spiders to help keep nature in balance. Spiders eat many insects that harm plants. They also serve as food for other animals.

Tarantulas do not attack people. Tarantulas are shy and will hide if people come near. Tarantulas only bite when they sense they are in danger. People can avoid being bitten by learning more about how tarantulas behave.

People need to preserve land for wild tarantulas. Then tarantulas can continue to play an important role in the natural world.

Spiders eat many insects that hurt plants.

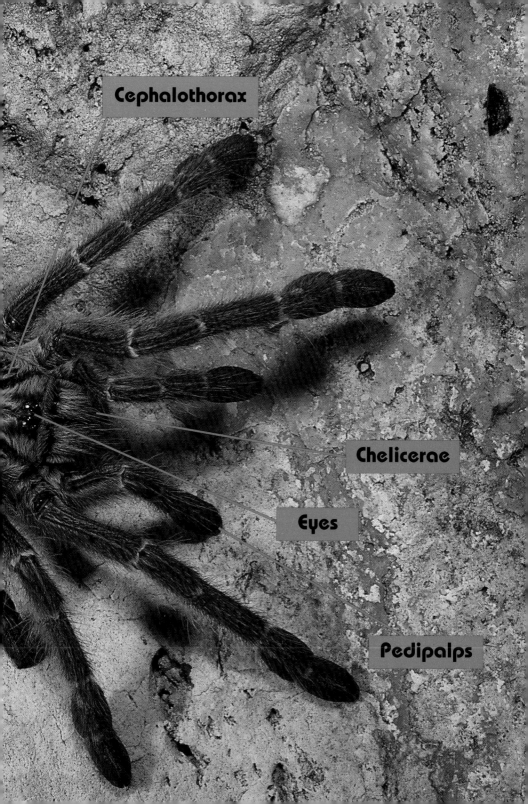

Cephalothorax

Chelicerae

Eyes

Pedipalps

Words to Know

abdomen (AB-duh-muhn)—the rear part of a tarantula's body

burrow (BUR-oh)—a hole in the ground dug by an animal for a home

cephalothorax (se-phuh-luh-THOR-aks)—the head and middle part of a tarantula's body

chelicera (ki-LI-suh-ruh)—a body part by a spider's mouth that is used like a jaw

exoskeleton (eks-oh-SKEL-uh-tuhn)—a structure on the outside of an animal that gives it support

fang (FANG)—a long, pointed tooth with a small hole in the end

molt (MOHLT)—the process of shedding the exoskeleton and growing a new one

nocturnal (nok-TUR-nuhl)—active at night

spiderling (SPYE-dur-ling)—a young spider

stridulation (stri-juh-LAY-shuhn)—a hissing noise made by rubbing hairs together

venom (VEN-uhm)—a poisonous liquid produced by some animals

To Learn More

LaBonte, Gail. *The Tarantula*. New York: Dillon Press, 1990.

Penny, Malcolm. *Discovering Spiders*. New York: The Bookwright Press, 1991.

Sanford, William R. and Carl R. Green. *The Tarantulas*. Mankato, Minn: Crestwood House, 1987.

Tesar, Jenny. *Spiders*. Woodbridge, Conn.: Blackbirch Press, Inc., 1993.

Useful Addresses

The American Tarantula Society
P.O. Box 3594
South Padre Island, TX 78597

The Smithsonian Institution
Office of Elementary & Secondary Education
Smithsonian Institution
Washington, DC 20560

West Coast Zoological
P.O. Box 16840
Plantation, FL 33318

Internet Sites

The American Tarantula Society Page
http://www.cowboy.net/~spider/ATS.html

Arachnology
http://www.ufsia.ac.be/Arachnology/
   Arachnology.html

Doug's Tarantula Page
http://www.concentric.net/%7EDmartin/index.shtml

Popular Pet Tarantulas
http://inetc.net/Tarantulas

Tarantulas@nationalgeographic.com
http://207.24.89.70/features/97/tarantulas/
   introframe.html

Index